WHEN COWBOYS RODE THE CHISHOLM TRAIL

in the late 1800's, they braved many dangers while driving herds of longhorn beef cattle over the 600-mile trail from Texas to Abilene, Kansas. Here is the story of the exciting though lonely lives these men led.

The hardy sights and sounds of a real cattle drive, including shrill cowboy yells, the bawling of cattle, and pounding of hooves on the trail are given life and action in this fascinating account. Also included are dangerous river crossings and attacks from Indians and Jayhawkers, or outlaws and cattle thieves. Here, too, is the true story of the one thing a cowboy feared most of all—a stampede.

In this book, readers follow the exciting lives of the men who drove the Backward Seven herd over the Chisholm Trail in 1870, traveling at the rate of about 15 miles per day. In good weather and bad, the drive continued over the rough route through wild, open country. At the end of the long drive the cattle were loaded onto the railroad freight cars which would carry them to prosperous northern markets.

This book is part of the *How They Lived* series, designed to give young people a wider and more comprehensive view of American history, and thus a deeper understanding and more lasting appreciation of their heritage.

When Cowboys Rode
the Chisholm Trail

When Cowboys Rode the Chisholm Trail

BY JAMES McCAGUE

ILLUSTRATED BY GEORGE LOH

GARRARD PUBLISHING COMPANY
CHAMPAIGN, ILLINOIS

Picture credits:

Amon Carter Museum, Fort Worth, Texas: p. 82

Art Division, New York Public Library: p. 9

Culver Pictures: p. 26 (all), 33, 68

Denver Public Library: p. 70–71

Gilcrease Institute: p. 11, 66

Historical Pictures Service: p. 20

Montana Historical Society: p. 24

Montana Historical Society, Mackay Collection: p. 1, 42, 58–59

Kansas State Historical Society, Topeka: p. 14 (all), 29, 37, 45, 64, 74, 89

Library of Congress: p. 77, 79

Picture Collection, New York Public Library: p. 5, 47

Rare Book Division, New York Public Library: p. 87, back cover

Whitney Gallery, Cody, Wyoming: p. 49

Collection of James R. Williams: p. 50

Woolaroc Museum, Bartlesville, Oklahoma: p. 2

Endsheets: "Trailing Texas Cattle" by Frederic Remington. From *The Frederic Remington Book* by Harold McCracken (Garden City, New York: Doubleday, 1966)

Contents

1. The Brush Poppers

Bill Blocker was only nineteen years old, that spring of 1870. But he had been doing a man's work for a long time. Bill was a tall, strong youngster. Texas boys grew up early in those days.

Quietly, with every sense alert, he rode his wiry cow pony through a dense thicket not far from the Pedernales River. In his right hand he held his *reata*, a 30-foot lasso of braided rawhide leather. It was coiled and ready. Near him on both sides rode other cowboys, though he could not see them through the thick underbrush.

Mesquite and chaparral bushes covered the ground in a tangled mass. Prickly cactus plants grew as high as a man's head. Their sharp spines clawed at the broad leather leggings, or chaps, which Bill wore. Sometimes he had to bend low in the saddle to avoid the gnarled branches of thorn trees stretching over the narrow trail.

Texans called this wild growth "blackjack." It made the going very rough. But hiding in the thicket were longhorn cattle, as wild and wary as deer. Bill Blocker and the other cowboys were hunting those cattle.

All at once there was a loud snort, a crackle of breaking branches. Right in front of him, Bill caught a glimpse of black-spotted, brown hide and huge, sweeping horns. It was a full-grown steer, big and lean and long-legged. Off it went, crashing through the brush at a furious pace.

Bill galloped in pursuit. All about him he heard commotion. The other cowboys had "jumped" some cattle too.

In an instant the blackjack was alive with noise and confusion. Shrill cowboy yells, the bawling of the cattle, and the pounding of hooves filled the air.

Swinging his reata around his head to make a wide loop, Bill flung it out ahead. In spite of the overhanging trees, his aim was true. The noose at the end of the reata dropped over the steer's horns. Instantly, Bill whipped the other end of it around his saddle horn. With a tug of the reins, he drew his horse back on its haunches.

The sudden stop jerked the big steer off its feet. It hit the ground with a thud.

Before the dazed animal could recover, Bill leaped out of the saddle. He had to be quick. The steer was fighting mad now—"on the

This cowboy and his horse plunge over dangerous foothills to capture their prize, a balky steer.

prod," as the cowboys said. If it once got up and caught him on foot, it would charge. And its long, sharp horns were terrible weapons.

Working swiftly, the young cowboy pulled three of the steer's hooves together. He yanked a short piece of rope from his belt, wound it around the steer's legs, and tied it in a tight knot. The steer was hog-tied now; it couldn't get up, no matter how hard it struggled.

But there was no time to waste. Other cattle were still crashing through the underbrush ahead. Quickly unfastening his reata from the steer's horns, Bill leaped back on his horse and dashed after them.

All through the thicket, the other cowboys were chasing cattle too. The longhorns were as fast and nimble as jackrabbits. They twisted and dodged in all directions. But the well-trained cow ponies turned and swerved as they followed every move.

Cactus and thorn trees tore at the men. Time and again they were nearly knocked from their saddles by low-hanging branches. But these fellows were all experienced "brush poppers." They knew what they were doing. The rough going couldn't stop them.

When cattle and cowboys tangled in a roundup, even horses could not keep their footing. Charles Russell painted this scene and called it "Jerked Down."

In some places the brush grew so thickly that it was impossible to throw a reata. Then a cowboy had to ride right up beside the steer he was chasing. Leaning down, he caught hold of its tail. He twisted the tail around his saddle horn and spurred his horse ahead in a burst of speed.

11

Up went the steer, lifted end over end in a mighty somersault. Down he went in a cloud of dust. Then he too was hog-tied and left.

The cowboys called this "tailing." It was cruel and hard on the poor steer. But chasing longhorns in a blackjack thicket was hard, dangerous work at best. No true brush popper could afford to be tenderhearted. And a Texas steer was pretty tough. He could take a lot of punishment.

At last most of the cattle had been caught.

A few had escaped. Now the cowboys and their weary horses could take a brief rest.

They needed one. About this same time, in another part of Texas, a young man by the name of James Cook was just learning to be a cowboy. A long time afterward he wrote a book called *Fifty Years on the Old Frontier*. In it he told how he felt after his first day of brush popping.

> "My clothing was pretty well torn off; also a goodly portion of my skin. About nine kinds of thorns were imbedded in my anatomy. I was ready for camp. So were our horses. But horses were cheap, and men could be hired, at eight dollars a month, who enjoyed the work."

The hog-tied steers were left where they lay for a while. Sometimes they were allowed to get onto their feet. Then they were tied to a tree by their horns and left there for several hours, or even a day or two. This was a little easier on them. But it was pretty sure to take some of the wildness out of them.

They still were far from tame. They never

A captured steer is held securely with ropes while a cowboy burns his outfit's brand into the steer's hide. A close-up of a branding iron is seen above and a few well-known brands, below.

would become really tame, in fact. But when they were untied, they could usually be driven to the corral, a sturdy pen which the cowboys already had built to hold them.

In this way, as the days passed, a herd of about a thousand cattle was gathered together. The work never stopped. And there was much more to it than just catching the cattle.

Many of the steers already had brands, the identifying marks of ranch owners, burned into their hides with a hot iron. The men who were making up the herd would have to pay the owners for these steers. The usual price was only about five dollars.

Many steers never had been branded, however. Cattlemen called them mavericks, and they belonged to whoever caught them. But at the corral all animals, branded or not, had to be roped and hog-tied again. Then their own special road brand was put on them.

The road brand for Bill Blocker's herd was a large figure seven, turned backward. That brand would keep the cattle from getting mixed up with other herds moving north.

And it would be a long road. This Backward Seven herd was going up the Chisholm Trail to Abilene, Kansas, more than 600 miles away.

2. Hard Times in Texas

Young as he was, Bill Blocker had managed to borrow enough money to buy a share in the Backward Seven herd. It was a great gamble, but Bill had plenty of grit and determination. He knew what it was like to be poor.

Most people in Texas were poor, in those long-ago years. The hard, bloody War Between the States had ended in 1865. Texas, a southern state, had been on the losing side.

Many Texans had gone off to fight for the South. Some had been killed. Many of the men who finally made their way back were wounded. All of them were weary. Their clothes were ragged and worn out. They were glad to be home again, where mothers and wives or sweethearts had waited through four long, worrisome years.

But they found hard times waiting too.

Their farms and ranches were neglected and rundown. Their tools were rusty or broken. Many of the best horses had been taken away to the war also. Money was scarce. About all that these Texans had left was their cattle.

It cheered them up a little to see that the cattle had done very well indeed.

Longhorns were a hardy breed. They were descended from the cattle first brought to America by Spanish explorers, many centuries earlier. There was an old saying that a long-horn could "live on air and scenery." And it was true that they could eat almost anything and get along on very little water.

With their owners away at war, these cattle had simply run wild. They had grown and multiplied at a great rate. Nobody knows how many of them there were in Texas by the time the war ended. Few cattlemen even tried to count their own herds. The trouble was, they were almost worthless.

Before the war, many Texas cattle had been

slaughtered for their hides alone. But now, with so many to be had, the price of cowhides was very low. There was more than enough beef to feed all the folk in Texas. Besides, nearly everyone had his own cows. So beef could scarcely be given away.

Disgusted ranchers used to say that "a man's poverty is measured by the number of cattle he owns." The more cattle he had, the poorer he was!

Strangely enough, at the same time the people in northern towns and cities needed beef as they never had before. The war had made them prosperous. They had good jobs in shops and factories.

To supply the need, big meat-packing plants had been started in Chicago, Illinois; St. Louis and Kansas City in Missouri; and in many other cities. These plants couldn't get enough cattle, even though they offered good prices.

A young man named Joseph McCoy thought about this sad state of affairs. It seemed to him that he saw a great opportunity there.

During the war, northern businessmen had begun to build railroads across the vast plains of the West. By 1866, the Union Pacific had almost crossed Nebraska Territory. Farther

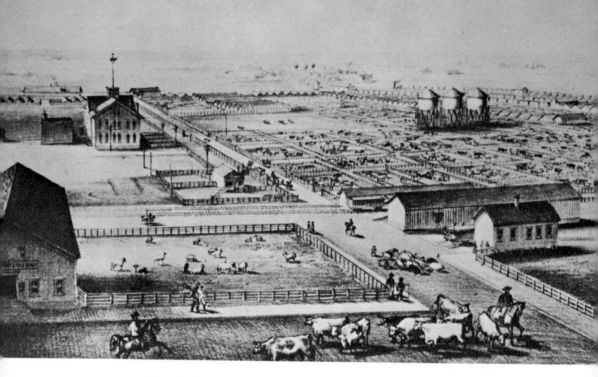

Joseph McCoy hoped to ship Texas longhorns to these
stockyards in Chicago on the Kansas Pacific.

south, workmen were laying tracks for another
railroad, the Kansas Pacific, across the state
of Kansas.

These railroads, thought McCoy, could easily
carry Texas cattle to market. The cattle would
have to be driven a long way to reach the
railroads, of course. But he was sure that
it could be done. Joseph McCoy was not a
Texan. He came from Illinois. But he was a
cattle buyer by trade. Most important, he had
imagination.

He talked with the men in charge of the Kansas Pacific Railroad. At first they doubted that they could make much money hauling cattle. But Joe McCoy wasn't a man who gave up easily. He kept talking. Finally, the railroad men agreed to put in switches and a sidetrack at the tiny Kansas town of Abilene.

McCoy went there. He had a big loading corral built beside the track. He bought a device called a Fairbanks scale, on which to weigh cattle when they were sold. Then he hired some men and sent them south. Their job was to urge Texas cattlemen to take their herds to Abilene.

Texans had driven trail herds north before this. Most of them had followed a route known as the Shawnee Trail, which ended in Missouri. But there were Indians and bandits along the way. They had often killed the cowboys and stolen the cattle.

Farther north, in Missouri, there were settlements. People there objected to having cattle driven over their farmlands. Sometimes they had banded together and refused to let the trail herds pass. So, all in all, the Shawnee Trail had not worked out very well.

Abilene lay far to the west of most settle-

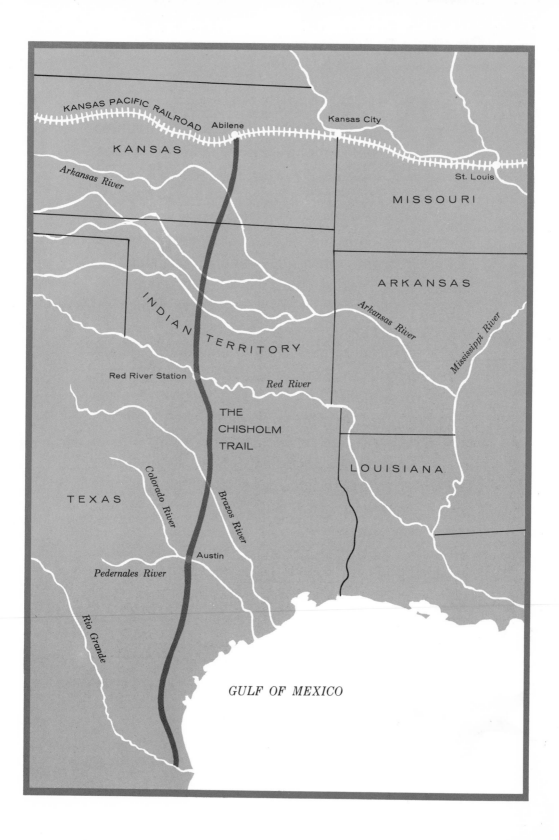

ments, however. The country was wild and empty and wide open. There were Indians and outlaw gangs there, too. But there also was another trail.

United States Army Scouts had found it many years before. Later an old Indian trader had driven his wagon trains over it. His name was Jesse Chisholm. Thus, in time, it came to be called the Chisholm Trail.

It was not a road. Far from it. The Chisholm Trail was nothing but a rough route across the country. There were no bridges over the many rivers that had to be crossed. No signposts showed how to go. Trail drivers would have to rely on scattered landmarks along the way.

Nevertheless, the Texans listened to Joe McCoy's men. They really had very little choice if they wanted to sell their cattle. A few of them decided to take a chance.

The first herd went up the Chisholm Trail in 1867. It got through safely. The cattle brought a good price in Abilene. Each year after that, more and more herds from Texas went plodding north to the railroad.

Soon now, the Backward Seven would be on its way.

3. The Trail Herd

One of Bill Blocker's older partners had been chosen as trail boss. He was a busy man as the starting day drew near.

The trail boss was always a good cattleman—usually one who had made trail drives before. He had to be a strong leader, for his word would be law on the long road north. He would drive his men hard. But he would have to be fair, too, in order to keep their respect.

His first job was hiring a trail crew. A herd

the size of the Backward Seven usually needed ten cowboys, or hands, besides the cook. The trail boss selected them very carefully. Every man had to know his business, of course. But it was wise to pick men who would get along with each other as well.

The crew would be living and working and facing hardships together. No shirkers or troublemakers were wanted.

The pay for a good trail hand was thirty dollars a month. The cook got the same.

Young Bill himself would serve as one of the hands. He wouldn't have things a bit easier than the rest, even though he was part-owner of the herd. This was included in his agreement with his partners.

Nearly all the hands were young. Hard work had made them tough and sinewy. Most had been soldiers in the War Between the States. Some might be Mexicans. A few probably were "drifters"—restless fellows who had no homes and simply wandered about the cattle ranges seeking adventure.

All we know about the Backward Seven crew are a few stories told later by some of Bill Blocker's friends. But we can take it for granted that it was much like all trail crews.

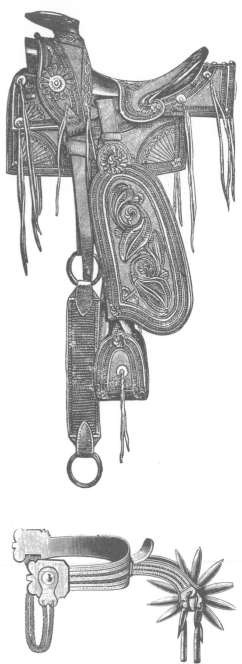

With his lariat and whip in hand and his gun at his waist, this cowboy is prepared for any trouble that may arise on the trail. A typical Western saddle and spurs are pictured.

Each man had his own saddle, chaps, and other gear. He took along just the clothes he wore: high-heeled boots with big, fancy spurs; rough work trousers and coat; a flannel or calico shirt. He wore a broad-brimmed felt hat. A big handkerchief, called a neckerchief, was tied around his throat.

Every hand had an oilskin slicker for rainy weather. He usually called it a "fish." He supplied his own blanket, or bedroll. His rifle was carried in a case, or boot, strapped to his saddle. He was seldom without his six-shooter pistol in its holster on his belt.

These things were all that many cowboys ever owned.

After the crew was hired, there still was much to do. Supplies were bought. Gear was checked and mended. The last of the cattle were road-branded. The *remuda*, a herd of horses for the trail hands, was selected. There had to be six horses for every cowboy.

The men would change horses often as the drive went along. In that way, fresh ones would always be ready when they were needed. And good cow ponies were important. They were chosen as carefully as the cowboys themselves.

While the men got ready for the drive, the cattle had to be turned out of the corral to graze. The hands rode around the herd, alert for trouble. The road-branded steers still were quite wild. They would try to run away, or stampede, at the slightest chance.

But at last, one morning in April, 1870, all was ready. There was no ceremony about starting. In that rough country around the Pedernales River, few wives or families were on hand to say good-bye.

Bill Blocker went first. He would ride the right point, ahead and a little to the right of the herd. He rode out slowly and quietly, to avoid scaring the cattle—or "spooking" them, in cowboy talk.

"Ho, cattle! Ho, ho, ho, ho," he chanted in a sort of singsong.

Slowly, one by one, a few steers followed him. Another cowboy rode up on the left point. He stayed even with Bill, a little to the left of the herd. Working together, the two point riders would keep the cattle headed the way they wanted them to go.

More steers began to follow the leaders. They bellowed and rolled their eyes and swung their great horns from side to side. But they kept going. Now, on both sides, two riders called swing men took their places behind the points.

Presently all of the cattle were moving, strung out in a long, straggling procession. Clouds of dust boiled up from the trampling hooves.

Two more riders, the flank men, fell in behind the swing men. All of the riders stayed some distance away from the herd, however. Nobody shouted or waved his arms, for cattle always were especially spooky when a drive was getting underway.

Now and then a steer snorted, tossed his head, and started off to one side or the other. Each time, a swing or flank man trotted up to head him off and turn him back into the herd. That was what they were there for.

At the tail end of the herd rode a couple of cowboys "on the drag." It would be their duty to keep the slower and weaker cattle moving, so that none fell behind and got lost.

In the meantime, the horse wrangler had started the remuda on its way. As a rule, the youngest and least experienced trail hand was picked for wrangler. He was in charge of the spare horses, herding them along on one side or the other of the trail herd.

Last of all, back at camp, the chuck wagon was ready. Stowed under its canvas top were provisions, a few simple tools, and the cowboys' bedrolls. Tied securely to one side was a big barrel filled with water. Built across the rear end of the wagon was the chuck box, a big cabinet that held the cook's pots and pans and tin dishes.

Underneath hung the "cooney." Sometimes it was also called the "caboose." It was just a rough cowhide fastened to the bottom of the wagon by its four corners, to make a kind of

sack. Firewood and various odds and ends were carried there.

The cook already had hitched up the mule team that would pull the chuck wagon. A trail cook had to be a good driver, or mule-skinner, in addition to knowing how to cook. When he saw the herd moving, he climbed up on the wagon seat. He shouted and slapped the reins on the mules' backs.

With a jingle of harness the chuck wagon pulled out, jolting and rattling over the rough ground.

The cook was in a hurry. He swung the wagon around the plodding herd in a wide half-circle. He had to get a good distance ahead, for he would be expected to have a hot meal ready for the crew when the time came to stop for the night.

The first day's drive had started.

4. Longhorns

The trail herd made a grand sight as it moved over the rolling Texas prairie.

Horns tossed and swung in a regular rhythm. Through the swirling dust almost every color under the sun could be seen. Some longhorns were black as coal. Others were brown, gray, even pure white—or any shade in between. Many were brindled, or spotted.

The bawling of the cattle and the thudding of thousands of hooves on the grassy earth filled the air with a low, steady roar.

Off at the sides the cowboys jogged along, slouched loosely in their saddles. The drag riders tugged hat brims down over their eyes. They pulled their neckerchiefs up over their mouths and noses, to keep from breathing the thick dust. That dust made riding drag a most unpleasant job.

But as the drive went on, the drag men would change places now and then with the flank or swing riders. Thus they would get a little relief.

None but fullgrown cattle were taken on most of the early trail herds. Cows with young calves were left behind, because the calves would not be able to keep up. But the fullgrown animals themselves varied a great deal.

It would have been a good idea, of course, for the men buying cattle for a trail herd to pick only the youngest, choicest animals. Those would bring the highest prices at Abilene. But Texans had a point of honor about that.

Any man who refused to take the cattle as they came was known as a "skinflint" or a "short sport."

The result was that many an old mossyhorn, twenty years old or more, went along too. The cowboys called them mossyhorns because their horns became wrinkled and rough as they grew older. Their tempers grew surlier, too. They were "tough to eat and tougher to handle," as the trail hands said.

It made no difference. They all would wind up as beef.

Old-time Texans had all sorts of words for their cattle. They might call them "critters," "cow brutes," or "ladinos," a Spanish word that meant "crafty" or "sly." And that word, by the way, tells us a good deal about a longhorn's disposition.

More often though, the cattle were just called beeves—the plural of beef.

These beeves were not at all like the fat, gentle cows we see on farms today.

They were alert, active animals. Their bodies were long and lean and tough. Seen from directly in front or behind, a longhorn looked tall but very thin and narrow. Sometimes a big steer grew so long that he sagged in the middle, and became swaybacked. The hides of these cattle were coarse and rough, their hooves as hard as iron.

The most remarkable thing about them, however, was their huge, sharp horns.

These descendants of the first longhorns still roam in the National Wildlife Refuge in Oklahoma.

Usually, these swept up from a steer's head in long, graceful curves. Occasionally they grew straight out on both sides. A few might be twisted like corkscrews. Horns five or six feet wide from tip to tip were fairly common. Stories have been told of some that were nine feet wide, or even more.

During the first few days of a drive, some steer that was bigger and smarter than the rest was likely to become a leader. This was so with the Backward Seven herd. And the leader turned out to be the big spotted steer Bill Blocker had roped back in the brush near the Pedernales River.

Bill began to notice that this steer always took the lead. He would jog along so close to the right point that the young cowboy could reach out and rest his hand on the tip of one horn. The steer didn't seem to mind.

Bill grew fond of him. He gave him a name: Pardner.

Pardner never became a pet, however. He still was wild and mean, ready to stampede anytime he took it into his head. But because the other beeves followed him, he made it easier to control the herd.

One of the strange things about longhorns was that they could get as homesick as human beings. The beeves didn't like to leave their home range. So they were driven hard for the first three or four days. This tired them out, and "broke them in" to the trail.

Before long, both men and cattle had settled down to their long journey.

5. Texas Lullaby

"Chuck-away!" shouted the cook. "Come and get it!"

He wouldn't call more than once, and the cowboys knew it. They tumbled out of their blankets in a hurry. It was long before dawn, still pitch-dark except for the flickering light of the campfire. But the trail crew's day had begun.

The men had slept on the ground around the chuck wagon. They hadn't undressed for bed, except to pull their boots off. No one bothered to wash his hands or face or comb his hair, either. Blankets were quickly rolled up and tossed into the chuck wagon.

In a very few minutes, everybody was lined up at the chuck box while the cook heaped their tin plates with food.

Breakfast, cooked over the open campfire, was a simple meal. There were biscuits baked in a big iron pot with a lid, covered with hot coals from the fire. It was called a Dutch oven. The cook had fried beefsteaks and made gravy. He had brewed a big pot of hot, black coffee.

Cowboys liked their coffee boiled until it was good and strong. An old trail-camp joke said that a cook was supposed to toss an iron horseshoe into the pot. If it didn't float, the coffee wasn't ready.

The men ate squatting on the ground around the campfire. They didn't waste any time about it. Overhead, stars still glittered in the black sky. But the trail boss was impatient to get started.

As soon as they had finished, the men went to the rope corral near the chuck wagon. The wrangler had already driven the horses of the remuda into it. This corral was just a rope strung on a big circle of sticks poked into the ground. The horses could have broken out of it easily, but somehow they never did.

An uninvited guest upsets the camp cook's breakfast
in Charles Russell's painting "Bronc to Breakfast."

Each man picked out the horse he would
ride that morning. He saddled up and mounted.
After a night's rest, the high-spirited cow
ponies often felt frisky. They bucked for a
while, trying to throw the men off. But they
never succeeded.

Away the riders went, to take their places
around the herd.

Two men who had been riding night guard
came in now. They gulped down their break-
fasts while the rest of the crew got the cattle

started. With a great clattering and banging, the cook washed his dishes and closed the chuck box. He hitched up his mules.

The sun was just peeping up over the eastern horizon, flooding the prairie with clear, rosy light.

For the first couple of hours the herd moved slowly. The beeves were allowed to graze as they went along. Then, gradually, the cowboys began to hurry them up until they were going at a brisk pace. The trail boss rode here and there about the herd, making sure that everything was in order and helping wherever he might be needed.

Now and then, one of the point riders galloped ahead to see that the way was clear. Whenever he did, the swing man on that side speeded up and took his place.

There often were rough stretches to be crossed—thickets, or steep gullies, or hilly, broken country. The point rider had to find the best way through such stretches, or around them. If he came to a river, he had to pick out the best place for the herd to wade or swim across.

This was one reason why the point men had to be top hands. And we may be sure that young Bill Blocker was proud to be riding point for the Backward Seven.

At noon, if there was a stream or pond handy, the herd was stopped while the beeves drank their fill. If there was no water, they went thirsty. Then once more they were allowed to graze or lie down during the hottest part of the day.

The cowboys took this opportunity to change horses and "wolf a bait" at the chuck wagon. That meant gobbling a quick snack of cold biscuits and beef. If they were lucky, some of them might even take a short nap in the shade of the chuck wagon.

About the middle of the afternoon, the herd was started again. This time it was driven hard until dusk. Then one of the point men rode ahead and selected a bed ground with good grass. There the beeves could graze for a while before they lay down for the night.

If all went well, a herd could make about fifteen miles a day.

Supper was practically the same as breakfast. Once in a while the cook might be able to buy some vegetables from ranches or trading posts along the trail. He tried to get potatoes and onions if he could. Then he would make a stew for the men. But most of the time the meals on a trail drive were pretty monotonous.

After supper the trail boss chose two men to take the first turn at night guard. The cook, the horse wrangler, and the trail boss were the only ones excused from this duty.

The night guards got fresh horses and rode out to the herd. The others might sit around the fire for a while, smoking and telling stories or playing cards. But after the long day in the saddle, they soon were ready to roll into their blankets with their boots for pillows.

The campfire died down to dimly glowing coals. Nothing could be heard but the snores of the tired men. Perhaps, far out on the prairie, an owl hooted or a coyote howled mournfully.

Out on the bed ground, the two night guards rode slowly around the herd. They would do this for two hours. Then two more men would take their places. And so it would go all through the night.

The night guards rode in opposite directions, passing each other each time they made the full circle. They might stop and talk for a moment then:

"How's it going, Slim?"

"Fine, Bill. They're layin' quiet."

Then they rode on. As they rode, they sang softly. The cattle seemed to like hearing men sing. It helped to keep the herd quiet. It also let the beeves know that the men were near, so that they never were startled when a rider loomed up out of the dark.

The songs usually were slow and sad. They had titles like "Old Hundred," or "Little Joe, the Wrangler," or "I'm A-Leadin' Ol' Dan." One of the favorites was "The Texas Lullaby." It had no words at all. A cowboy would make

Frederic Remington painted this night guard keeping
watch over the herd on a starry night.

words up as he rode along. And they generally came out in a long, quavering wail:

Wo-up, wo-up, get along you ol' rascals,
Get along, get along, wo-up, wo-o-o-o. . . .

The nights were lonely, and time passed slowly. When their two hours were over at last, one of the night guards rode into camp and woke up the next two men. They rode out and took their places around the herd.

The first two usually stopped to have a cup of coffee from the pot which was always kept warm on the campfire coals. Then they turned in. The strong coffee never kept them awake. They were much too tired.

Thus, the days and nights followed one another. Each day was much like the one before. The Backward Seven herd plodded on. Then one day it began to rain.

And with the rain came trouble.

6. Red River Station

Day after day the rain came down. The ground grew soft and muddy underfoot. The cowboys rode along, hunched in their yellow slickers with water dripping from their soggy hat brims.

For some reason, rain always made a herd "drift." The cattle kept wanting to stray away from the trail. Point, swing, and flank men had to ride furiously up and down, trying to straighten them out and turn them back in the proper direction. But the wet beeves were stubborn. It was slow, hard going.

The nights were miserable. No tents were carried on a trail drive. The cook was lucky, for he could make his bed in the chuck wagon. But everyone else had to sleep right out in the pelting rain.

Blankets and clothing were soaked. The leather of the men's boots swelled and stiffened with the constant wetting. Then, if a man took his boots off at night he could scarcely get them back on the next morning. So many of the cowboys never took off their boots at all. But that was uncomfortable, too.

Thunder and lightning often came with the rain, making the beeves nervous and spooky.

The cook tries hard to keep his fire lit on a rainy morning in camp. Painting by Charles Russell.

The men riding night guard had to be doubly alert for signs of a stampede starting. Sometimes the whole crew had to keep riding around the restless herd all night long.

Weariness and lack of sleep made the trail hands grumble. But no one thought of quitting.

The weather was still bad when the Backward Seven herd arrived at Red River Station. It was not much of a settlement— just a few shacks and log cabins huddled around a trading post on the south bank of the broad, muddy Red River. This river was the northern boundary of Texas.

Red River Station was the place where the trail herds always crossed. But the rain had swelled the river to a raging, swirling flood.

Uprooted trees with great, jagged branches swept past. Now and then the body of some drowned animal floated by. Massed along the bank of the river were several other trail herds. Their trail bosses had decided that trying to cross now would be too dangerous. They were waiting for the water to go down.

The Backward Seven's trail boss agreed with them. He gave orders to pitch camp and hold the herd where it was.

A day or two passed. Holding the herd was

dull work. Being wet and miserable had been bad enough before. But it was worse to be standing still, getting nowhere. And the rain didn't stop. The river still was high and swift.

Finally, Bill Blocker went to the trail boss. "If you put me in charge of the herd, I'll take it across," said he.

We can only guess what the trail boss thought of that. He probably had his doubts. But Bill did own part of the herd. He was a top hand, besides. And the trail boss himself was tired of waiting.

"All right," he said.

Boldly the young cowboy snapped out his commands. The herd was driven back to the south for a few miles. Then it was swung around and headed for the river once more. This gave the men time to get the beeves strung out as they usually were on the trail, so that they didn't crowd one another.

Bill rode in his regular place on the right point. Beside him was the big lead steer, Pardner. Straight down the sloping river bank they went. Side by side, they waded into the water. The strong, chilly current swirled about them. A few more steps, and both horse and steer were swimming.

The herd followed. Longhorns were good swimmers. Nevertheless, a herd often balked at going into such a rough, dangerous river. But these beeves never hesitated.

Nothing could be seen above the water but a long, straggling line of heads and horns. The current pushed the line far downstream. The beeves could make little headway against it. At any moment they might be swept together in a kicking, struggling mass.

If that happened, there would be panic. The weaker cattle would be forced under the water and drowned. Most of the herd might be lost.

Still on their horses, the cowboys swam
along on both sides. But there was little they
could do to help the cattle. It took all their
strength just to keep going themselves.

At the head of the line, Pardner swam on.

Bill's horse almost went under. He slipped
out of the saddle and swam beside it. His
boots and his heavy chaps dragged him down.
He splashed desperately, clinging to the horse's
tail with one hand. Water filled his mouth
and nose, choking him. Still he hung on.

At last he felt bottom under his feet. He
saw Pardner scramble up the river bank ahead.

Bill and his horse stumbled after him. The dripping beeves followed, struggling up onto solid ground. One by one, the other riders and their horses reached shore.

Behind the herd came the horses of the remuda. Then the chuck wagon went lurching and swaying down to the river's edge. The last few cowboys on the south bank had tied big logs along both sides, making the wagon into a kind of clumsy raft. The mules, still hitched to it, were driven into the water. Bobbing and rocking, the chuck wagon floated along behind.

It was swept far downstream also. But at last the mules reached shallow water. Some of the cowboys who already had crossed rode out into the stream. They tied their reatas fast to the wagon, so that the sturdy cow ponies could help the mules to pull.

Straining and tugging together, they hauled the chuck wagon up onto the north bank.

Men, horses, and cattle were tired and bedraggled. But Bill Blocker had kept his promise. The Backward Seven was across the Red River. They had left Texas behind them now. Ahead lay long miles through the vast Indian Territory.

7. Across The Nations

Today, the great state of Oklahoma lies across the Red River from Texas. In the 1870's, though, all the land from the river northward to Kansas had been set aside for the Indians by the United States government.

It was called The Nations for short, because most of the tribes living there were known as the Five Nations. These were the Cherokees, Choctaws, Creeks, Chickasaws, and Seminoles. They came from the states east of the Mississippi River. But they had given up their lands there in return for these western lands.

They were peaceful Indians. Many had taken up the white men's ways. They owned farms and ranches, and were good, hard-working people. But there still were some wild tribes roaming about, as well. And they were likely to make trouble. A large band of such Indians was pretty sure to ride up to any herd on the Chisholm Trail.

They usually were a hard-looking lot. Some wore old, ragged shirts or hats, or other articles of white men's clothing. Others were

In "Toll Collectors" by Russell, a band of Indians demands cattle in exchange for safe passage.

wrapped in dirty blankets. Several of the Indians carried guns.

When they saw them, the cowboys reached for their own guns. One of them shouted a warning. The trail boss came galloping up.

But the Indians usually stopped some way off. Their chief rode forward. He waved his arm toward the herd.

"Wo-haw!" he cried. "Wo-haw! Chuck-away!"

Any experienced trail boss knew what that meant. "Wo-haw" was a word the Indians

used for cattle. This band was hungry. They
wanted a steer to eat. And if they didn't get
one, there was no telling what they might do.

By this time, more of the trail hands had
trotted up. They scowled and kept their hands
close to their gun butts. Texans didn't like
Indians. Many of these men could remember
times, not so many years before, when fierce
Kiowa and Comanche Indians had raided the
ranches back home.

But the trail boss didn't want any trouble.
He nodded to the chief. "Cut out a beef for
them," he told some of his riders.

The cowboys always chose the poorest, skin-
niest old steer in the herd, and drove him out.
But the Indians were satisfied. They killed the
steer. They got busy skinning him and cutting
up the meat. The trail herd went on its way.

It was better, after all, to give up one
scrawny steer than to fight a pack of hungry
Indians. And in a way, it was only fair. This
land belonged to the Indians. Most trail bosses
didn't mind paying to cross The Nations.

There was always a chance that they would
get their fill of fighting before long, anyway.
Worse men than Indians lurked along the trail
to Abilene. There were Jayhawkers.

To this day, people who live in the state of Kansas are often known as Jayhawkers. It is just a friendly sort of nickname now. But to a Texas trail hand in those days, the Jayhawkers were outlaws and cattle thieves.

Some of them were hard, evil men who claimed that they had fought for the South during the War Between the States. Perhaps they had, but they just used that as an excuse for their crimes. Gangs of such men sometimes raided trail herds. They killed any cowboys who tried to stop them. Then they drove the cattle off for themselves.

Most Jayhawkers, though, were sneaky, cowardly fellows. A story handed down among old-time cattlemen tells us how they worked— and how much the Texans hated them.

There was a small creek in a certain rough, brushy part of The Nations. It was a wild, lonely place, and trail herds always seemed to stampede there. Something would scare the beeves and away they would go, running pell-mell. Then, when the herd finally was rounded up again, several beeves were always missing.

This went on for a long time. Nobody could figure out why. But at last a trail boss named Bob Mitchell grew suspicious. He rode ahead

for a good look when his herd drew near that
creek. And sure enough, something caught his
eye.

A man was crouched in the bushes beside
the creek, ready to jump out and spook the
cattle when they came along.

No cowboy in that trail crew ever told
exactly what happened next. But the herd
crossed the creek without stampeding. And
when it had passed, there was the Jayhawker,
hanging by the neck from a stout tree limb
at the side of the trail. Those Texans were
hard men, too. But all they ever said was:

"He hanged himself, so he wouldn't stompede any more cattle."

"Stompede" was the way Texans always pronounced the word.

As far as we know, the Backward Seven crew had no trouble with Jayhawkers. But like all crews, they had to be prepared if trouble came. At night the men slept with rifles and pistols close at hand. The older cowboys always spread their bedrolls on the hardest, most uncomfortable ground they could find.

They advised the younger men to do the same. That way, they explained, a man would not sleep very soundly. He could wake up, ready for action, in an instant.

If a man riding night guard grew too sleepy, he sometimes stuck a pinch of tobacco up under his eyelids. It made the eyes terribly sore, but it kept a man awake.

Jayhawkers were not the trail crews' only worry. No matter how it started, the stampede itself was the thing they feared most. Almost anything—a sudden gust of wind, a loud noise, any unexpected movement—might stampede the spooky longhorns. The most common cause of all was a thunderstorm.

And that spring of 1870 was a stormy one.

8. "Stompede!"

Some nights the trail hands could feel a stampede coming.

Such a night usually was very still. It was *too* still. The air felt thick and heavy. The men riding night guard could feel an odd, unpleasant prickling on their skins.

Back at camp every cowboy had saddled his best horse. The best horses always were picked for night work. Each man had tied his horse close to his sleeping place, so that he could jump up and into the saddle without delay.

Out on the bed ground, the cattle seemed quiet enough. But now and then a steer would get up and roam restlessly about for a few minutes. He might crop some grass and then lie down again.

Away off in the northwest, thick clouds drifted up across the sky. Thunder rumbled in the distance. Once in a while lightning flickered, faint and far away. A storm was brewing. But perhaps it would pass on to the southward. The night guards hoped so. Just to be ready, though, they put their slickers on.

The clouds grew thicker. Before long the night was so black that nothing could be seen, even a foot or two away. Still it was quiet. The night guards could hear each other singing as they rode slowly around the herd.

"Oh-h-h-h-h-h, bang the drum slowly and play the fife lowly," sang one. "Those words came low-w-w-w-w and mournfully. . . ."

That song was called "The Dying Cowboy." It sounded sad and weird in the deep black stillness. The men longed for their two-hour stint to end.

All at once, little balls of dull, pale light appeared on the tips of every steer's horns. This often happened just before a thunder-

"Stampeded by Lightning" by Frederic Remington

storm. It was called fox-fire, or will-o'-the-wisp, or sometimes St. Elmo's fire. It was caused by electricity in the air. But it was a ghostly, frightening thing to see.

Then, suddenly, a brilliant, blue-white flash of lightning split the sky. A mighty clap of thunder shook the earth. Before the echoes could die away, they were drowned by the louder thunder of thousands of hooves.

Nothing could stop the beeves. The night guards rode for their lives, trying to stay out of the way. They slackened their reins and

66

let their horses run. A good cow pony could find its way through the black night far better than any man.

Ahead might be deep gullies or ravines, hidden by the darkness. There were holes that could trip a horse and break its leg, sending the rider crashing to the ground. If they were caught in the herd, both horse and man would be dragged down and crushed under those thundering hooves.

More lightning flashes showed a sea of tossing horns and wild, bloodshot eyes. Big raindrops pelted down. The storm broke in its full fury. Now the wet horns and the riders' slickers gleamed in the lightning flashes. Thunder pealed, crash after crash, like a hundred cannons firing.

Around the chuck wagon in camp, the other hands had awakened at once. They needed no one to tell them what had happened.

"Stompede!"

Leaping into their saddles, spurring their horses to top speed, they dashed after the herd.

The best way to handle a stampede was to turn it. The cowboys rode hard to get up on the right or left point of the herd. They yelled and waved hats and slickers at the beeves. Galloping along at a breakneck pace, they crowded in close to the leading steers, trying to force them to turn away.

Then, gradually, the whole herd might begin to mill, or keep going around in a great circle, until the beeves wore themselves out and stopped running. But milling didn't always work out very well.

Now the lightning flashes showed the cattle mixed up in wild confusion. Horns clashed and rattled together. Some steers reared up and tried to climb over others in their panic. Some went down, and were trampled to death in the milling mass.

That was bad. Dead cattle would bring no money at Abilene.

"Let 'em scatter," the trail boss roared.

But once it was started, a mill was hard to break up. Cowboys rode boldly into the herd, trying to separate the maddened beeves. Sometimes a man had to draw his pistol and shoot steers that threatened to rip his horse open with their great horns.

Often, in the midst of this, a herd stampeded again without warning.

But at last the storm ended. The sun rose, and daylight was very welcome to the bruised and tired men. The herd might be scattered for miles in every direction. Now it had to be rounded up again.

No one rested until that was done. It might take all day, or even several days, but no one would stop to rest or eat until the herd was back together. Stampedes, too, were part of a trail hand's job.

And once in a while, when the trail boss counted his crew, one of the cowboys was not there. Hearts grew heavy then. Every man could guess what that meant. Somewhere along the trail left by the stampeding herd, they would find the missing man—or what was left of him.

Probably no one ever would know how it was that he had been caught under the churning hooves. But each man knew very well that the same thing might have happened to him.

A few words and a crude grave along the trail marked the burial of a cowboy trampled by the herd.

A grave was dug with a spade from the chuck wagon. The men gathered around. They took off their hats. If the trail boss could remember a verse from the Bible, he recited it. If not, he tried to think of something good to say about the dead man. The funeral did not take long.

With his knife, one of the cowboys carved the man's name on a bit of plank for a grave marker.

Then, solemnly, the men mounted their horses. They started the herd moving. Abilene still was a long way off.

9. The Last Camp

Many weeks had passed. It was summer now. The Indian Nations had been left behind, and the Backward Seven was in Kansas. But the broad, rolling prairie still looked much the same.

The outfit was showing signs of wear and tear. The chuck wagon was battered and creaky. Broken spokes in the wheels were tied together with strips of rawhide. Dried and hardened by the sun, the rawhide was as strong as iron.

The trail hands' clothing was ragged, worn, and caked with dust. Their hair had grown long and tangled; their faces were dirty and unshaven.

In spite of stampedes, Indians, Jayhawkers, and dangerous river crossings, however, not many beeves had been lost along the way. This was a great tribute to the skill and bravery of the cowboys—and to the toughness of the longhorns themselves.

But everyone was getting pretty tired.

Then, one day a strange sound drifted down the prairie wind. Perhaps some sharp-eared cowboy heard it first. He cocked his head and listened. There it came again—the faraway tooting of a locomotive whistle.

"Boys, it's the railroad!" he cried.

Maybe Bill Blocker rode ahead to take a look. He stopped at the top of one of the long prairie ridges. He peered north, squinting his eyes against the sun.

He could see Abilene.

It was not a very big town, though it sprawled over a fairly large area. Even from a long way off, it looked gray and somewhat shabby. Flimsy wooden buildings straggled along its wide, dusty streets. Most of the buildings were only one story high. But some had ugly, square false fronts which made them look taller.

Standing out above all the rest was a big, three-story hotel. Joe McCoy had had it built for the cattlemen who came to Abilene. It was called the Drovers' Cottage.

Through the town ran the tracks of the Kansas Pacific Railroad. They stretched off into the distance to east and west. And beside the tracks, out on the edge of the town,

Abilene in its heyday as a cow town boasted a busy hotel, Drovers Cottage, and a thriving railroad.

was Joe McCoy's corral. It was big and strong enough to hold three thousand steers. A line of cattle cars stood on the sidetrack nearby.

We cannot say for sure how the men of the Backward Seven got their first look at Abilene. But it was something like this, certainly. And it must have been a grand sight to the cowboys after their weeks on the trail. Abilene was the end of the journey. Soon their hard work would be over.

The herd was driven to its last bed ground, a few miles from town. Other trail herds grazed on the prairie not far away. The Kansas grass was rich and good. The beeves could be held there as long as necessary. A herd sometimes had to wait its turn if the corral was already full of cattle.

The cook lighted his campfire. He opened the chuck box and got busy mixing up a batch of biscuits for supper. The trail boss rode into Abilene to Joe McCoy's office. That was where he would find the cattle buyers.

No record remains to tell us how soon the Backward Seven herd was sold, or how good a price it brought. But Bill Blocker's share was enough to pay back the money he had borrowed, with some left over. He had made a good start as a cattleman.

There was one last, sad moment. Pardner, the big spotted steer, still led the herd when it was started off the bed ground and driven into the corral. Bill was sorry to see him go. He and Pardner had been together a long time, it seemed. Now it was good-bye.

But there was no place for soft hearts in the cattle business. Bill was nineteen—already a man. Just the same, it may be that he swallowed a lump in his throat when he turned away.

The beeves were counted as they went through the corral gate. Each was driven onto the big Fairbanks scale and weighed. After a while, a huffing, chugging engine would pull a train of cattle cars up to the loading chute. They would stop there, one by one.

Bawling and bellowing, the beeves would be driven up a sloping passageway into the cars. When every car was loaded, the engineer would give a blast on the whistle. Smoke would gush from the tall, diamond-shaped smokestack. Clanking and jolting, the train would roll slowly down the track, heading east.

Swinging braided lariats, cattlemen drive a herd of
longhorns into a cattle car in Abilene.

But none of that would concern the
Backward Seven men. As soon as the cattle
were in the corral, their work was done.

The cattle buyer had watched carefully
while the beeves were counted and weighed.
Then he and the trail boss went to Joe
McCoy's office. There the trail boss signed a
bill of sale for the cattle. The buyer counted
out the money he had coming.

When the boss rode back to camp, it was
the trail crew's turn to be paid off.

The drive had lasted about three months. Thus each man had earned about ninety dollars. It was little enough to show for all their hard work and discomfort, the sleepless nights, and the many dangers they had faced.

But all that was forgotten now. To the simple, rough cowboys, ninety dollars seemed like a fortune. They were in fine, high spirits as they lined up at the chuck wagon for their money. They laughed and joked and played good-natured tricks on each other as they got ready to ride into Abilene.

Now it was time to have some fun.

10. First of the Cow Towns

Whooping and yelling in sheer high spirits, the cowboys raced each other into town.

Abilene was the first of the famous cow towns of the West. The trail herds from Texas had made it a busy and prosperous place. Besides the Drovers' Cottage, there were three smaller hotels. There were five large general stores. They sold groceries, hardware, clothing —and just about anything else a cowboy might think of buying.

Very few trail hands ever stayed at a hotel, however. Such fancy places were fine for ranch owners, trail bosses, and well-to-do cattle buyers from the East. But the cowboys were looking for excitement, not comfort.

There were ten saloons in town. And most of the men pulled up and got down off their horses at the first one they saw. No whiskey or other strong drink had been allowed in the trail camps. Now they were eager to "wash the trail dust out of their throats."

Next, they probably looked around for a barber shop. In those days, in towns like Abilene, the barber shop was the only place where a cowboy could get a bath.

In a room at the back of his shop, the barber usually kept a big wooden tub and a stove for heating buckets of water. For about twenty-five cents, the trail-weary cowboy could fill the tub, get in, and scrub himself with a bar of strong soap.

After a three-month cattle drive, there was no doubt that he needed a good scrubbing. Then, after a shave and a haircut—with plenty of sweet-smelling hair tonic doused on his head—he started out to see the town.

Possibly he stopped in at one of the stores. There he could buy a present for his mother, sister, or sweetheart back home. He might

pick out a pretty ribbon for her hair, or a
new calico dress. If he wanted to be a real
dude, he might even buy a suit of "store
clothes" for himself.

But many of the wild fellows from the Texas
brush country scorned that sort of thing. They
usually headed straight for Texas Town. That
was the part of Abilene that lay south of the
railroad tracks.

It was a rough, poor section. Most of the
saloons were there, along with gambling dens
and loud, gaudy dance halls. Those were the
only places where a cowboy looking for a good
time could go.

The people who lived in Abilene liked the money the Texans spent there, but they didn't like the Texans themselves.

The cowboys swaggered about the streets in their high-heeled boots, with fancy spurs jingling. They wore their gun belts and six-shooters everywhere they went. The hard life on the trail had made them rough and violent in their ways. The Abilene folk were a little afraid of them.

Some cowboys *were* pretty quick to reach

This painting by Charles Russell of cowboys shooting up a cow town is called "In Without Knocking."

for their guns when they had had too much whiskey to drink. Then shots could be heard all over town. Bullets whizzed through the air. Frightened people ran to get out of the way.

Actually, however, the bullets seldom hit anyone. Most of the stories told about gun fights in Abilene were made up later. Rowdy and wild as they were, the cowboys really did very little harm. Nevertheless, some leading citizens decided that they needed a town marshal to make the Texans behave. So they hired one.

On the Fourth of July, 1870, Tom Smith arrived in Abilene.

His nickname was Bear River Smith. He was a red-headed Irishman with blue eyes and a big, bushy mustache. Though he wasn't a very big man, he was strong and quick. But the most remarkable thing about him didn't show up for a few days.

Bear River Smith put up signs in all the stores, saloons, and public places in town. They forbade anyone to carry guns in Abilene. The Texans didn't like that a bit. And one of them, a cowboy named Big Hank, thought that the marshal was bluffing.

No one remembers Big Hank's last name,

or the outfit he worked for. But he was evidently tough and brave. He met Bear River Smith in the street, face to face, and dared him to take his gun away.

Strangely enough, the marshal never reached for his own gun. Instead, he stepped in quickly. His fist darted out—straight to Big Hank's jaw. Down went the cowboy in a heap. He was knocked unconscious.

When he regained his senses, Bear River Smith ordered him quietly to get out of town at once. And Big Hank did. He had had enough.

The other Texans were amazed and bewildered when they heard what had happened. The idea of a man fighting with nothing but his fists was new to them. But it was plain that they couldn't shoot a man who refused to draw his own pistol. That would be murder. It would be cowardly, besides.

There just didn't seem to be anything they could do about Bear River Smith. They had to respect him, though. One more cowboy tried to beat Smith. He too was knocked out. After that there was no more trouble.

No one found out, until a long time later, that Tom Smith had once been a policeman in

New York City. It was there that he had
learned to box so well.

For all we know, the Backward Seven men
were in Abilene at this time. Perhaps some of
them got acquainted with Bear River Smith.
Whether they did or not, however, they didn't
stay in town long. They soon ran out of
money. Only a few cowboys, like Bill Blocker,
were smart enough to save what they earned.

The rest wasted their money, buying whiskey or playing cards. Then there was nothing to do but head south, back down the Chisholm Trail. It would be a long, hard ride. But at least they had no trail herd to take care of now. No one would have to ride night guard or worry about stampedes.

By November, Abilene was a dull and quiet place. The last of the trail herds had come. The beeves had all been sold and shipped away. The last of the trail hands had headed homeward. Now there would be very little happening until the next summer.

Then it would all begin again.

11. Trails' End

As the years passed, many thousands of cattle beat the Chisholm Trail into a roadway several hundred yards wide. It stretched across the plains like a great scar, trodden down by hooves and rutted with chuck-wagon tracks.

Every spring, all through the 1870's and the 1880's, Texas trail herds headed north. The first ones started as soon as the grass grew green enough to make good grazing along the way. All summer long, and on into early fall, other herds followed.

One year, around the middle of the 1880's, a Texas cattleman named Ike Pryor drove 45,000 beeves over the Chisholm Trail. They were divided into herds of about three thousand each. The herds followed one right after another, just a few miles apart.

Pryor employed more than 165 trail hands. Altogether, the remudas totaled a thousand horses. The beeves alone were worth more than a million dollars. And Ike Pryor was only one of many cattlemen who traveled the trail that year. Trail driving had become big business.

In all those years, hardly anything was done to improve the Chisholm Trail. In some places, big mounds of earth were piled up to make crude trail markers. But no one bothered to build bridges over the rivers. The beeves swam or waded across, as they always had. A trail hand's life was still as hard and dangerous as ever. Other changes took place, however.

In Kansas, settlers kept moving west. Most of them were homesteaders, or small farmers. The cattlemen called them sod-busters, because they plowed the land and planted crops. They built fences to keep the trail herds from trampling through their fields and ruining the crops.

Soon the rough and ready, trail-riding cowboys gave way to farmers who fenced in the land. This Kansas family was photographed in front of their sod home.

Gradually, the trail drivers had to swing farther and farther west in order to get through. In a few years, trail herds no longer went to Abilene.

Ellsworth and Hays City, also on the Kansas Pacific Railroad, became wild, rough cow towns in their turn. But other railroads were being built all over the West and Southwest now.

Before long another trail, the Western, was opened up. It ran many miles west of the old Chisholm Trail. Over it, herds were driven to Dodge City, Kansas; Ogallala, Nebraska;

Cheyenne, Wyoming; and other towns. They all became famous cow towns, too.

In time, the new railroads reached down into Texas. Yet cattlemen clung to their old ways.

In the year 1884, a meeting of ranch owners was held at St. Louis, Missouri. During the meeting, someone suggested that the United States government should set aside land for a National Cattle Trail. It would be six miles wide, with fences on both sides. And it would run all the way from the Red River to Canada.

The cattlemen thought this was a wonderful idea. A short time later, at Washington, D.C., a Texas congressman by the name of Miller tried to get the United States Congress to pass a law creating such a trail. But Miller's bill never was passed.

It was just as well. The great days of trail driving already were coming to an end.

A new breed of cattle, called Herefords, was being introduced on the Texas ranges. Herefords grew fatter and heavier than the tough, stringy longhorns. Thus they brought more money when they were sold. There was more profit in raising them.

And so, slowly but surely, the new breed began to replace the herds of longhorns.

Herefords were not nearly as hardy as long-horns, however. Their hooves were softer. They could not walk as fast, or as far. Such cattle could not stand the long, hard trail drives.

The last trail herd that we know of went up the Western Trail to Wyoming in 1896. A man named John McCanles was the trail boss. He got his herd to its destination. But he had such a hard struggle that no one else ever tried to follow him.

It had become much easier, and better in every way, to ship cattle by rail.

Today, the lordly longhorn is almost gone. A few small herds remain, here and there. Most of them are kept by wealthy cattlemen for sentimental reasons. One of the finest herds roams over a National Wildlife Refuge in the Wichita Mountains of southwestern Oklahoma.

As for the old Chisholm Trail, it is now a modern, paved highway called U.S. 81. It runs through fertile, prosperous farmlands and busy cities. Comfortable motels and good restaurants stand beside the road. The rivers are crossed by broad, strong bridges.

Trucks and automobiles roll up and down the highway. Some of the trucks are loaded with fat, placid cattle on their way to market. Times have changed since old Pardner led the Backward Seven herd up the dusty trail with young Bill Blocker riding point.

Glossary

blackjack: the Texans' word for thorny thicket growth

brand: a mark burned on the skin with a hot iron; also, to mark with a brand

chaps: leather coverings worn over trousers by cowboys to protect their legs

chuck wagon: wagon equipped as a kitchen for feeding cowboys

cooney: a piece of cowhide tied like a sack under a chuck wagon to carry odds and ends

corral: a place fenced in for holding horses, cattle, etc.

cow town: a town which is a cattle center

drag riders: hands who rode at the end of the herd to keep the slow and weak cattle from falling behind

drifter: one who goes along in an aimless way

flank men: hands who rode behind the swing men to the side of the herd

fox-fire: an eerie phosphorescent light sometimes seen on the tips of the cattle's horns

hand: a person who is hired to work with his hands

hog-tie: to tie the four feet of an animal

Jayhawker: an outlaw or cattle thief

maverick: an animal which has not been branded

mossyhorns: old cattle

muleskinner: a man who drives mules or horses

point riders: trail hands who rode slightly ahead and to the side of the herd

rawhide: cattle hide that is not yet made into leather

reata: a long lasso of braided rawhide

remuda: a herd of horses used by the trail hands

St. Elmo's fire: another word for fox-fire

sod-buster: cattlemen's name for homesteaders or small farmers

spook: a word used by cowboys meaning to scare

stampede: a sudden rush of a herd of cattle; also, to move in such a rush

steer: any male of cattle raised for beef

swing men: hands who rode behind the point riders to the side of the herd

The Nations: the land between the Red River and Kansas, set aside in the 1870's by the U.S. government for the Indians

will-o'-the-wisp: another word for fox-fire

Wo-haw: the word the Indians used to mean cattle

wolf a bait: cowboy talk meaning to have a quick snack

wrangler: a trail hand, usually the least experienced, who was in charge of the spare horses on a drive

Index